AF131443

BOOK ANALYSIS

By Jule Lenzen

The Grass is Singing
BY DORIS LESSING

Bright
≡Summaries.com

DORIS LESSING

ENGLISH NOVELIST AND SHORT STORY WRITER

- **Born in Kermanshah, Persia in 1919.**
- **Died in London in 2013.**
- **Notable works:**
  - *The Golden Notebook* (1962), novel
  - *This Was the Old Chief's Country* (1951), short story collection
  - *Under My Skin* (1994), autobiography

Born in Persia to English parents, Doris had one younger brother, Harry. As a child she lived first in Persia, then in England, and finally in Southern Rhodesia (now Zimbabwe), where her father started a farm. She never received a formal education. She was highly outspoken about her political views, which also deeply influenced her writing, and always had a cause that she supported. She left home in 1937 and worked in Salisbury (Harare, Zimbabwe), where she married Frank Charles Wisdom, already pregnant by him. They had two children together but divorced in 1943. Doris, by that point, was deeply engaged with the communist movement (but later broke with it) and married the leader of the communist group, the German Jewish refugee Gottfried Lessing, in 1945. They had a son, Peter, but divorced in 1949. She had been publishing stories and poems in journals already and left Southern Rhodesia with Peter in the same year, eventually settling in England. In 1950, the first of her 26 novels, *The Grass is Singing*, was published. Lessing was exceedingly successful during her lifetime, receiving many prizes and honorary degrees. In 2007 she finally received the Nobel Prize for Literature, shortly after the publication of her novel *The Cleft*. She was highly experimental in her writing and wrote realist novels as well as science fiction. One of the main influences on her writing was the philosophy of Idries Shah (Sufi author and teacher, 1924-1996).

THE GRASS IS SINGING

SETTLER NARRATIVE SET IN SOUTHERN RHODESIA

- **Genre:** novel
- **Reference edition:** Lessing, D. (1994) *The Grass is Singing*. London: Flamingo.
- **1st edition:** 1950
- **Themes:** colonialism, Africa, settler society, poverty, postcolonial studies, racism

The Grass is Singing was Lessing's first novel and was immediately successful. She took the manuscripts with her when she left Southern Rhodesia in 1949. In the novel, she explores language as a means of oppression of the black population in Southern Rhodesia (Maslen, 2017: 3). Lessing was uneasy about the treatment of the country's black African population (*ibid.*: 2).

Strong autobiographical tendencies can be detected in the novel: it is set in the rural farm environment of Southern Rhodesia where Lessing grew up. Her father's life's dream was to take up farming, and so he ventured to do so but was highly unsuccessful, and the family had to be very economical. Moreover, Lessing saw her parents' marriage as proof of the destructive effects of marriage for marriage's sake upon the independent mind of her mother (*ibid.*).

The narrative of *The Grass is Singing* centres around the lives of Dick and Mary Turner, who live on a farm in Southern Rhodesia. Dick is unskilled at farming, and there is therefore no chance for the two to escape the poor circumstances in which they live.

SUMMARY

The first chapter of the book foreshadows the end: it recounts, from various outsider perspectives, the murder of Mary Turner. It is made clear that the Turners' native houseboy committed the crime, but that there is more to it than meets the eye. Tony Marston, the assistant who lives on the farm with the Turners, tries to convince the Sergeant and Charlie Slatter, a neighbour, of this fact. These two quickly shut him up, however, as what he has to say could have negative effects on the dominant white society in the country.

MARY MEETS DICK

In the second chapter of the novel, the upbringing and life of Mary Turner are described. Her parents have spent all their lives in South Africa, and so has she. She grows up in various small villages across the country, where her father works as a pumpman on the railway. She has no fond memories of her childhood: she only remembers the constant fights between her parents and the poverty. Eventually it will become clear that she was also sexually abused by her father. When she comes of age Mary moves to a town in South Africa where she leads a highly independent, but also impersonal life – she seems to be detached from herself. She is jolted out of her stupor by an overheard conversation between her friends, who make fun of her for not being married at over 30 and for still dressing like a child. This deeply hurts and unsettles Mary, and she tries to find a husband. However, she always shies away from any intimate relations with men. Dick has been a farmer in southern Rhodesia for a while when he meets Mary by chance on a day out in the city. He realises how lonely he is, and eventually asks her to marry him. Mary accepts, although she does not seem to be fully aware of the life of poverty that awaits her.

SETTLING IN ON THE FARM

Mary receives a shock when she arrives at Dick's farm: she was not prepared for the extent of poverty that awaits her. It reminds her horribly of the childhood she has tried to forget. Most devastating of all, the little house that Dick built on the farm has no ceilings, only a tin roof – meaning that it becomes unbearably hot during the day. At first, however, Mary tries to occupy herself in the house and enjoys her new freedom. Dick spends his days on the farm, supervising the natives doing the farmwork, and the only company Mary has in the house is that of a native cook. This soon leads to the first problems: Mary cannot deal with the natives or control her temper when coming face to face with them, so one after the other quits and it becomes increasingly difficult to find replacements. Moreover, she falls into a kind of lethargy – the heat is unbearable to her, and she refuses to help Dick on the farm. The only months that rouse her are those of winter, when it rains and is a bearable temperature. To crown Mary's disappointment, one of Dick's business ventures ends in installing a shop for natives on the premises which Mary is supposed to look after. This reminds her horribly of her childhood when these stores formed the centre of her unhappy life. In an impulsive move, Mary runs off back to the city, wanting to take up her life there again. This proves impossible, and for the first time she realises how much she has changed since her marriage. Dick takes her back to the farm, and at first their marriage seems to improve. Then Dick falls ill with malaria, and Mary has to look after him. There is little intimacy between the spouses as Mary does not like to be touched.

MOSES

Dick repeatedly asks Mary to look after the farm while he is ill, and she eventually caves in. She has to get the natives to work again, and in this, she takes a far more strict and violent approach than Dick. In one flight of temper, she strikes one of the workers, Moses, across the face with a whip – and for a short moment she is scared that he will hurt her as well. He does not, however. As a result of Dick's illness, Mary becomes very interested in the farm and soon finds out that Dick has little talent for farming and that, if nothing changes, they will never escape poverty. She attempts to convince Dick to run the farm more economically, and for a while this seems to be successful, but in the end, Dick relapses into old habits. This is the final push that sends Mary towards deterioration. She realises that she will never be able to live the life she wants, and that her circumstances will never improve. At the same time, Moses comes to work as a cook at the house. After one nervous breakdown in front of him, the power balance between the two shifts. Mary is increasingly dependent on him. This becomes obvious to Slatter, who visits them once. He realises that something needs to be done, and fears for the entire white settler community (as their position of power over the natives is what makes their way of life possible). He offers to buy Dick's farm and to send him and Mary on a holiday to recover. For four weeks an apprentice, Tony, lives with the Turners on the farm to learn how to look after it. He also witnesses the closeness between Mary and Moses – at one point he sees Moses dressing Mary.

MARY'S DEATH

The last chapter of the novel deals with Mary's last day – which is incidentally also her last day on the farm before the planned holiday and escape. The entire day she seems to know that she will die. At night she goes onto the veranda, where Moses finds her and kills her. In her last moment she feels disloyal to Moses. Finally, Moses' inner conflict is revealed in the aftermath of killing Mary. He eventually just waits to be arrested, instead of killing someone else as well.

CHARACTER STUDY

MARY TURNER

Mary grows up in South Africa as a daughter of English settlers. Her childhood is an unhappy one: she frequently witnesses fights between her parents as her father does not earn enough money and spends a substantial amount on alcohol. She is also sexually abused by her father, which only transpires in her adult life (p. 165). She originally has two elder siblings, both of whom die in the same year (p. 34). She then goes to a boarding school and is glad to escape the poverty once she is of age, and moves to the city, where she starts working in an office. She lives in a club with other girls and shows little grief when her parents die; in fact, she sees this as a new freedom. She has many acquaintances whom she calls her friends, male and female, and she often spends time with her male friends, but never has an intimate relationship. She is never alone and lives like this for many years, until comments by some of her friends that she overhears shake her out of her innocent happiness:

"'She's not fifteen any longer: it is ridiculous! Someone should tell her about her clothes.' [...] 'Why doesn't she marry? She must have had plenty of chances.' There was a dry chuckle. 'I don't think so. My husband was keen on her himself once, but he thinks she will never marry. She just isn't like that, isn't like that at all. Something missing somewhere.'" (p. 40)

The sentence 'She isn't like that' will resonate with Mary until the end of her life. The overheard conversation makes her feel inadequate and she tries to live up to her friend's expectations, which leads to her marrying Dick and returning to the life of rural poverty that she had escaped from. The independence she had gained is subsequently lost for lack of support.

On the farm there is little social contact and Mary spends more time alone than ever before in her life. She resents Mrs Slatter, one of her neighbours, for patronising her and making fun of her poverty; however, she mistakes genuine compassion on Mrs Slatter's side for more negative feelings (p. 76). Mary's feeling of having been betrayed by her friends lets her see enemies and falsity everywhere, and she is increasingly incapable of creating real bonds with anyone, be it on the level of love or friendship.

Mary's distaste and resentment voice themselves in her treatment of the natives, who anger her: she is prone to temperamental outbursts with them. Here, a strong racism is voiced. Life on the farm heightens Mary's mental fragility, and she slowly deteriorates into madness (p. 195). In the end, she has a nervous breakdown: she does not remember what she has been doing or saying and sinks into lethargy (p. 194).

With Moses, Mary develops an ambivalent relationship: she is dependent on him and at the same time scared of him, but she also feels a certain kind of fascination for him (p. 161). She is obsessed by the thought of him, which pushes Dick entirely from her mind (p. 167).

Mary seems to have no sense of self and is only occasionally awakened from the stupor she seems to spend her entire life in. She does not even ask herself questions about her own identity until she lives on the farm when she is already past the age of 30. Mary's clothing suggests that she never really left her childhood behind (p. 41): the abuse she experienced as a child has had the effect of her not proceeding past this development stage. Mary also pronounces that she needs the feeling of superiority to men to exist (p. 44).

DICK TURNER

Dick is a farmer in rural Southern Rhodesia. Five years before meeting Mary, he started his farm. He has little skill at farming, as Mary realises some years into their marriage, and therefore never manages to make any profit from it. On top of that, he is extremely unlucky. He has a great deal of imagination and lives in his dream world rather than the real world: he is often possessed by a passion for business ventures that are bound to fail, such as beekeeping, but he has a great enthusiasm for these. He also feels a great connection with the land and farms sustainably (p. 170).

He is as racist as towards the natives every other white person in the community, but treats the natives with forbearance: when one of the cooks steals some raisins, Dick merely remarks: "'He probably did, but he's a good old swine on the whole.'" (p. 64). Dick prides himself on having found the right strategy to motivate the natives to do his work just like the other white farmers in the district (p. 65):

> "He worked as only a man possessed by a vision can work, from six in the morning till seven at night, taking his meals on the lands, his whole being concentrated on the farm. His dream was to get married and have children. Only he could not ask a woman to share such a life." (p. 46)

However, Dick is very lonely, and he decides to marry Mary after having met her on a night out in town at the cinema. Dick has a very low opinion of himself. In his relationship with Mary he feels inadequate, but at the same time like he somehow deserves the cold treatment he receives from her – she can only stand him when she can pity him, and, if anything, has maternal feelings for him. Dick senses Mary's reluctance to have any sort of intimate relationship with him and is hurt by this. The spouses drift apart, and even though they live together they do not really form a unit.

Dick always tries to pay off his debts and takes out less money than any other farmer. However, his lack of talent for farming prevents him from ever making a profit. He lives from year to year but at some point simply acquiesces to his situation of poverty and gives up striving for bigger things. By the time Mary dies, Dick is "[...] incurably mad" (p. 16).

ANALYSIS

POSTCOLONIAL STUDIES AND *THE GRASS IS SINGING*

Postcolonial studies engage with the global effects of colonial rule on colonised societies, and also, albeit to a lesser extent, on colonisers. The novel can be classified as a settler narrative and deals with postcolonial concepts such as colonial discourse, hybridity and ambivalence.

SETTLER NARRATIVE

Settler narratives explore the impact of colonial rule on the coloniser. 'Settler' is in a way another word for 'colonist' – in the context of postcolonial studies, it describes Europeans who settle in European colonies (Ashcroft et al., 2007: 193). In her novel, Lessing critically engages with the complicated relationship between settlers and indigenous peoples, as well as the inhumane treatment of the indigenous population. This critical engagement and her outspoken criticism of apartheid (a series of laws legalising the segregation of black South Africans from 1948 onwards) were so controversial at the time that Lessing was banned from entering Rhodesia and South Africa in 1956 (Maslen, 2017: 3). In the context of postcolonial studies, settlers have a complicated standing: they are colonisers and colonised at the same time, while not belonging to either group completely:

> "Settlers are displaced from their own point of origin and may have difficulties in establishing their identity in the new place [...]. They are frequently constructed within a discourse of difference and inferiority by the colonizing power ('colonials/colonial') and so suffer discrimination as colonial subjects themselves. At the same time, they act as the agents of that power, and their own identity depends in part, at least initially, on retaining their sense of difference from the 'native' population." (Ashcroft et al., 2007: 194)

This sense of difference is most obviously established through colonial discourse and language and extensively thematised in Lessing's novel – this will be discussed in the next sub-chapter.

The Grass is Singing deals with the lives of settlers in southern Africa. Often, as in the case of Mary and Dick, these are born in the colonised country and grow up there, forming their own identity that is neither that of the 'native' nor that of the colonising 'home' country. However, these settlers retain a strong bond with the colonising home country:

> "[...] reading letters from home [...] – momentarily transported back to the country for which they were so bitterly homesick, but where they would never choose to live again: 'South Africa gets into you,' these self-exiled people would say, ruefully. For Mary, the word 'Home' spoken nostalgically, meant England, although both her parents were South Africans and had never been to England." (p. 32)

There is a significant difference in the ways Mary and Dick deal with their ambivalent situations as settlers. The outcome for both is the same, however: they eventually go mad, showing that the strain of living in between colonising powers and colonised communities is too much for them. Mary even affirms: "I have been ill for years [...]. Inside, somewhere. Inside. Not *ill*, you understand. Everything wrong, somewhere." (p. 201).

Dick, on the other hand, feels a great connection with the land he lives on: "He loved it and was part of it." (p. 123). This feeling of his is one of the reasons Slatter despises him: it aligns Dick more closely with the indigenous people of the land, which is what most settlers try to avoid in order to set themselves apart.

LANGUAGE AS POWER

In colonial times, the superiority of the white colonisers was established through something known as colonial discourse.

Colonial discourse

- Colonial discourse is a set of assumptions about the colonised people as seen by the coloniser (Europe and its Other). It is implicated in racism.
- It is an instrument of power.
- "Consequently, colonial discourse is the complex of signs and practices that organize social existence and social reproduction within colonial relationships." (Ashcroft et al., 2007: 37).

The use of colonial discourse is also portrayed in the novel. As has been said above, the settlers have a need to set themselves apart from the native population in order to establish their superiority. This is done through the perpetuation of some general assumptions about the native population by the settler society: the natives are portrayed as lazy, criminal, stupid, unreliable and inhuman. The native people are on the same level as animals as far as the white settler community is concerned.

This is shown most clearly with the newly arrived Tony Marston. He 'makes the mistake' of treating the native population as human beings, and is therefore not taken seriously by either Charlie Slatter or the Sergeant:

> "When old settlers say, 'One has to understand the country,' what they mean is, 'You have to get used to our ideas about the native.' They are saying, in effect, 'Learn our ideas, or otherwise get out: we don't want you.' Most of these young men were brought up with vague ideas about equality. They were shocked, for the first week or so, by the way natives were treated. They were revolted a hundred times a day by the casual way they were spoken of, as if they were so many

cattle; or by a blow, or a look. They had been prepared to treat them as human beings. But they could not stand out against the society they were joining." (p. 18)

Ambivalence

- Ambivalence is implicated in colonial discourse.
- "[...] it describes the complex mix of attraction and repulsion that characterizes the relationship between colonizer and colonized." (Ashcroft et al., 2007: 10).
- Ambivalence disrupts the authority of the colonising society as it unsettles the simple relationship between coloniser and colonised.

Arguably, this ambivalence is the major topic of the novel: Mary's relationship with Moses, in itself characterised by the ambivalence of repulsion and attraction, creates, on a larger scale, a disruption of the colonial discourse. By treating Moses as a human being, Mary and Moses' power relationship is reversed: Mary is at the mercy of Moses. This shows that the black community can regain power over their white colonisers, and this is also why Slatter and the Sergeant are afraid that Tony will speak out on the matter. Tony imagines what he could say to them:

> "If you must blame somebody, blame Mrs Turner. You can't have it both ways. Either the white people are responsible for their behaviour, or they are not. It takes two to make a murder – a murder of this kind. Though, one can't really blame her either. She can't help being what she is. […]" (p. 27)

HYBRIDITY

Hybridity is a concept that can be employed to describe the particular situation of settlers. The colonial discourse and its framework of colonialism establish clear binaries between the coloniser and the colonised, Europe and its Other. However, settlers do not belong to either category. Hybridity "[…] commonly refers to the creation of new transcultural forms within the contact zone produced by colonization." (Ashcroft et al., 2007: 108), and can therefore be used to describe the new cultural identity that settlers embody.

Lessing's novel shows how the in-between state of the settler is affected by living in between those categories. In the character of Mary, a binarity can be detected as Dick observes: "With him she seemed at ease, quiet, almost maternal. With the natives she was a virago." (p. 69). Interestingly, these two sides of her character show themselves in relation to white society and the native population. Increasingly, however, Mary develops a hybrid identity: in a conversation with Moses, she treats him as she would a white man: "'Don't be ridiculous. I am not afraid of you.' She spoke as she might have done to a white man, with whom she was flirting a little." (p. 166).

The novel also shows how Mary is only able to think in binary categories: in order to treat Moses as a human being, rather than as a savage, she has to forget about Dick, who represents the white settler society:

> "And he [Tony] began to understand with a horrified pity, her [Mary's] utter indifference to Dick; she had shut out everything that conflicted with her actions, that would revive the code she had been brought up to follow." (p. 187)

Mary articulates the feeling of being a settler and not belonging with either the colonising or the colonised society quite clearly:

> "[...] She was conscious of that gulf, but not as unredeemable alteration in herself. She felt, rather, as if she had been lifted from the part fitted to her, in a play she understood, and made suddenly to act one unfamiliar to her. It was a feeling of being out of character that chilled her, not knowledge that she had changed." (p. 97)

Mary always struggles to make sense of her situation (p. 195) but is unable to do so. In the end, the potent image of a cracking mirror, in itself standing for hybridity, is employed to describe Mary's feeling of not being able to make sense of her own situation: "The conflict between her judgement of herself, and her feeling of innocence, of having been propelled by something that she did not understand, cracked the wholeness of her vision." (*ibid.*).

FURTHER REFLECTION

SOME QUESTIONS TO THINK ABOUT...

- Why do you think Moses kills Mary? Explain your answer.
- What do you think makes Mary's position unique, in terms of her being a woman and a settler? Does she face struggles that the male settlers do not have to endure? If so, what are they?
- Consider how racism is imposed by the white society upon its members. Consider the cases of Mary and of Tony Marston in this context.
- How would you interpret Mary's vision of the farm's deterioration in the last chapter (pp. 195-196)? Explain your answer.
- "It is terrible to destroy a person's picture of himself in the interests of truth or some other abstraction. How can one know he will be able to create another to enable him to go on living? Mary's idea of herself was destroyed and she was not fitted to recreate herself." (p. 43)

Can this statement be adapted to colonial discourse, which creates a sense of self for the colonised society? Explain your answer.

- How does Lessing criticise the use of colonial discourse and the settler-native relationship as a whole? Use examples to illustrate your answer.
- What other possible interpretations are there for Mary's feeling that something has always been wrong with her (p. 201), apart from the implications of her position as a settler?
- Mary, before her death, expresses the feeling that she deserves to die. This is similar to Dick's continuous self-abasement. Do you think this is linked to their positions as colonisers? Explain your answer.
- Compare the novel to the 1981 film version. In the film, it is suggested that Mary and Moses have a love affair. Do you think this interpretation is believable? Why do you think this interpretation was chosen?

We want to hear from you!
Leave a comment on your online library
and share your favourite books on social media!

FURTHER READING

REFERENCE EDITION

- Lessing, D. (1994) *The Grass is Singing*. London: Flamingo.

REFERENCE STUDIES

- Ashcroft, B. et al., eds. (2007) *Postcolonial Studies: The Key Concepts*. USA and Canada: Routledge.

- Maslen, E. (2017) Lessing [*née* Tayler], Doris May. *Oxford DNB*. [Online]. [Accessed 25 January 2019]. Available from: <https://doi.org/10.1093/ref:odnb/108270>

ADDITIONAL SOURCES

- *Doris Lessing Studies*. [Journal].

ADAPTATIONS

- *The Grass is Singing*. (1962) [TV drama]. Owen Leeming. Dir. UK: BBC.

- *Killing Heat*. (1981) [Film]. Michael Raeburn. Dir. Zambia, Sweden: Chibote, SFI.

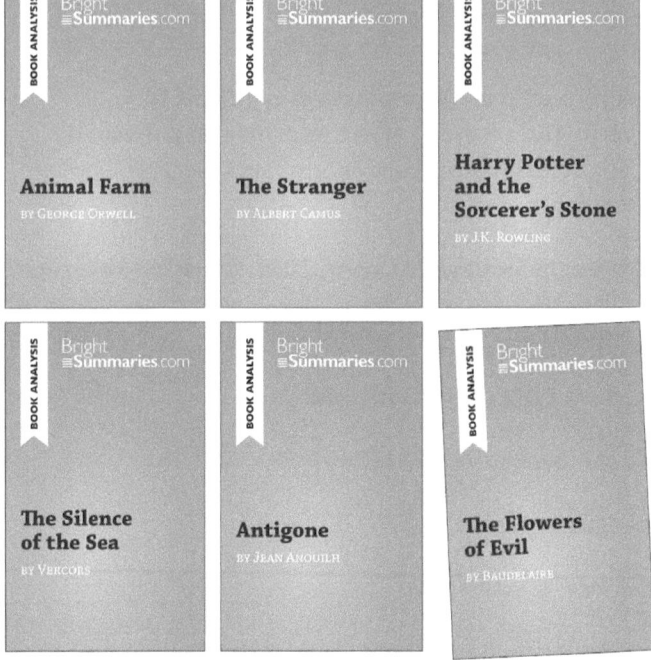

Although the editor makes every effort to
verify the accuracy of the information published,
BrightSummaries.com accepts no responsibility for
the content of this book.

www.brightsummaries.com

Ebook EAN: 9782808017985

Paperback EAN: 9782808017992

Legal Deposit: D/2019/12603/66

Cover: © Primento

Digital conception by Primento, the digital partner of
publishers.